CATSKILLS
COUNTRY
S T Y L E

First published in the United States of America in 2002 by
RIZZOLI INTERNATIONAL PUBLICATIONS, INC.
300 Park Avenue South, New York, NY 10010

ISBN: 0-8478-2468-3
LCCN: 2002090784

Front cover: Barbara Davis' House
Back cover: Joe Pescarino and Ed Mintiens' garden
p. 2: Kitchen in an abandoned house in the town of Gilboa
p. 3: Shelmandine house on Blenheim Hill
pp. 4-5: A rainbow over the dairy barn at River View Farm
p. 6: A trailer near the Ashokan Reservoir
p. 7: The Thomas Cole studio in Catskill
p. 10: Kaaterskill Creek at Palenville
p. 12: A view of the Hudson river from Olana
p. 15: A fawn under a clothesline in Schoharie
p. 16: Still life in the Shelmandine house
p. 19: An abandoned church in Breakabeen
p. 20: A playground teepee at Maplecrest Resort
p. 23: An uninhabited farmhouse in town of Broome
pp. 24-25: The "icicle" house in the village of Oak Hill
p. 26-27: Tourist cabins along Route 20 near Sharon
p.202: One of the many old apple orchards in spring
p. 204: A canoe behind tourist cabins on Catskill Creek
p.205: The Keogh Cabins in the resort town of East Durham

Design: Judy Geib and Aldo Sampieri
Project Editor: Kristen Schilo

Printed in China

2002 2003 2004 2005 2006 / 10 9 8 7 6 5 4 3 2 1

CATSKILLS
COUNTRY
STYLE

Steve Gross   Sue Daley

Introduction by Francine Prose

RIZZOLI
NEW YORK

CONTENTS

CATSKILLS COUNTRY

FRANCINE PROSE

My first experience with the Catskills came long before I had been there and even longer before I fell in love with the region and decided to make it my home: it came when I read the story of Rip Van Winkle, for which this region was the setting. Somewhere in the mountains, not too far (nor far enough!) away from New York City, where I grew up, a man (it seemed) had gone into the woods with his gun and his dog and encountered a sort of spectral bowling team—the ghosts of Henry Hudson and his crew. After accepting their friendly offer and sharing some of their potent home brew, Rip fell asleep and woke up twenty years later—an old man and a stranger in an alien world that had forgotten and moved past him.

I was a nervous, impressionable child; the story greatly disturbed me, even though I could hardly imagine what it might be like to live for twenty years, let alone how it might feel to lose two decades from one's allotted span thanks to a long, ill-advised nap. Of course, I couldn't have known that the story was a metaphor for the universal yet weirdly dreamlike experience of waking up one day and discovering that one is no longer young. Nor did it occur to me that Washington Irving's retelling of the folk tale had anything, really, to do with the Catskills—that is, with an actual place, a particular locale—except for Henry Hudson's Knickerbocker cameo appearance. Falling asleep for twenty years—couldn't that happen anywhere?

But only now, after living in the Catskills for roughly as long as Rip Van Winkle's sleep and after viewing the luminous and evocative photographs of Steve Gross and

Sue Daley, do I realize how beautifully the story expresses something very singular about a precise longitude and latitude, a specific place on the planet. To live or spend time in the Catskills is to experience a magical slippage, a funny little detour in the steady, apparently one-way march of time. It's easier here than in most places to find one's uncertainty: Is it today or twenty years ago, this century or the last?

In the homes that speckle its gorgeous landscape, and in the photographs collected here, the past seems powerfully present, and the present moment seems saturated with the past. And once we step away from civilization and venture across the fields and into the shaggy forests that climb up the mountainsides, the passing decades seem insignificant compared to what really matters—the seasons.

Perhaps this sense of being beyond the reach of time has something to do with the light—that absolutely unique Catskills light. It is quite unlike any other light, and recognizable anywhere. Of course, the light changes minute to minute, hour to hour, and day to day. And yet it's obviously unaffected by such details as what year it happens to be. The eternal nature of this particular light is why the naturalist John Burroughs' description of the overnight, miraculous change in the atmosphere that signals the sudden transition from winter to spring seems, eighty years after his death, like an accurate rendering of what we remember experiencing on a March morning in the recent past.

"A fitful, gusty wind was blowing, though the sky was clear. But the sunlight was not the same. There was an interfusion of a new element. Not ten days before there had been a day just as bright—even brighter and warmer—a clear, crystalline day of February, with nothing vernal in it; but this day was opaline; there was a film, a sentiment in it, a nearer approach to life."

—John Burroughs

Likewise, when people familiar with the region see a landscape by Thomas Cole and Frederick Church, they may experience a nearly vertiginous sense of disorientation and dislocation. How could the sky in that canvas look so exactly like the same dramatic expanse of the heavens that, on certain summer evenings, demands our attention and, with an almost magnetic attraction, pulls us out of doors, away from our kitchens and dinner tables? That same light suffuses the photos of Gross and Daley and this is why these pictures also manage to pull off the magic trick of looking so much like the place itself—to capture its clear and moody essence. Of course, the natural landscape itself—such as magical, almost legendary places like Kaaterskill Falls and Overlook Mountain—retains a sublime and romantic quality that recalls the lush extravagance of those early paintings. And vice versa.

In the Catskills, time relaxes its grip, which may be why so many of the interiors included in the present volume share a reckless (yet tasteful) disregard for the confining prison of a single historical style. The range and ambition of the public and private rooms at Wilderstein—the 1891 mansion not far from Rhinebeck and the banks of the Hudson River—insist on the house's right to invoke or approximate a style most closely suited both to each room's fantasy ambiance and its practical function: The library suggests the reading rooms of a medieval monastery; the parlor, the place where our colonial ancestors paid their social calls; and the drawing room, where French royalty could while away the pleasant hours beneath the cherubs disporting themselves on the ceiling.

Guided by the inspired hand of Candace Wheeler, the inventive late-nineteenth-century pioneer in the fields of textile and design, Pennyroyal—Wheeler's quietly spectacular "cottage" in the Onteora Park Colony—became a showplace of an aesthetic that married the homey, the natural, and the exquisite, and that combined an affection for the plain decor from the early history of this country with the very different ideal of simplicity practiced by the proponents of the Arts & Crafts Movement. And at Byrdcliffe, the utopian artists' colony that Hervey White and Ralph Whitehead founded near Woodstock, the Arts & Crafts aesthetic—a vision which found its inspiration in a romantic and heavily sweetened dream of the Middle Ages—directed everything from the architecture to the furniture, clothing, and behavior of the residents. At both Onteora Park and Byrdcliffe, social life included costumed rituals and pageants that recreated a past, part Classical Greek, part Celtic, part medieval—a composite, imaginary era that never existed.

Elsewhere in the region, artists (both formally schooled and self-taught) fashioned environments that not only slipped through the bonds of time, but also the limitations of nationality, culture, and what we think of as ordinary reality. Olana—to my mind, the most fascinating and gorgeous house in the region—represents Frederick Church's passionate and obsessive desire to relocate the splendors of the Alhambra and the Persian palace to the more verdant, peaceful landscape of the Hudson Valley; partly, what makes the result so enchanting is that it offers the visitor

a unique opportunity to see what might happen if the sensual indulgences of a Sultan's harem were refashioned to conform to the considerably more proper and self-conscious dictates of a nineteenth-century sensibility. Meanwhile, across the river, Otto Ziemer's "outsider artist" cabin between Woodstock and Kingston may be the ultimate expression of the home-as-art project, a highly individualistic and intensely energetic scheme of wild color and decoration that single-handedly reinvents the excessive and the rococo.

Which brings us back to Rip Van Winkle and to the possibility that his story represents yet another perception about the Catskills: A notion of the area as a place to which one can go and be transformed, an Eden from which one returns renewed and changed—possibly forever. Certainly, that dream underlies the appeal that has brought generations of vacationers and refugees from the stresses of the city to seek relaxation and recovery. No doubt some version of that was in the minds of the travelers who, in earlier eras, frequented the region's majestic grand hotels—the Catskill Mountain House, the Overlook Mountain House, and the Tremper House—as well as the humbler cabins perched up on the mountains and nestled in the valleys. And surely that was the ambition and the fondest hope of the immigrants who flocked to the bungalow colonies and later the resort hotels of Sullivan County; the peace, the greenery, and the quiet and relaxation were the physical evidence of America keeping its promise to the masses "yearning to breathe free." And those ailing in spirit and body who made their seasonal pilgrimages to take the waters at such health spas as Sharon Springs carried these dreams one step further and envisioned the Catskills as a place of healing.

In fact they were right, they were all right: Those who imagined that they had found the fountain of health and well-being; those who hoped that the mountains would restore them or transform them into their best and strongest selves; those who believed that they had found an unspoiled paradise far (in spirit, if not in miles) from the assaultive clamor and stress of the city; and those who understood that the Catskills would, if only briefly, liberate them from the prison of time. As those of us who live here now or who visit will discover—and as these handsome photographs make abundantly clear—the world of the Catskills follows its own rules, operates on its own time, and insists upon its own beauty.

J O H N
BURROUGHS'
C A B I N S

The rustic haven known as
"Woodchuck Lodge," built in the 1860s,
was a summer home to writer John
Burroughs, America's eminent essayist
and much-loved naturalist. With
panoramic views of the mountains near
the town of Roxbury, the "little gray
farmhouse" as he called it, hosted many
of Burroughs illustrious friends
such as Henry Ford, John Muir,
Thomas Edison, and Harvey Firestone.

Burroughs took frequent naps and sometimes spent the night out on the porch of Woodchuck Lodge. Many of the furnishings in his cabins were made by him and have a humble, unaffected simplicity. "The man that forgets himself, he is the man we like; and the dwelling that forgets itself . . . is the dwelling that fills the eye," wrote Burroughs.

In 1895 John Burroughs built another retreat for himself, called "Slabsides," as a place in which to write and study nature. The main room of the rough-cut slab-walled cabin remains much the way Burroughs left it, with his writing things arranged out on his desk and the table set for one of his many visitors.

Homespun striped fabric is part of the very simple handmade cabinet Burroughs crafted for himself in a corner of the lodge. The walking sticks must have been used on the nature rambles Burroughs always encouraged people to take. The family homestead on the quiet back road still has its rows of sugar maples, apple orchards, and stone fences.

A small room at the lodge contains an early phonograph that Thomas Edison gave to his friend John Burroughs. At Burroughs' funeral, Edison was there to adjust the hand-cranked machine. Burroughs is buried here next to his "Boyhood Rock" a contemplation spot overlooking Old Clump Mountain and the family farm where he was raised.

One can feel the gentle spirit of John Burroughs within the deep green walls of Woodchuck Lodge's main room. Like Thoreau, Emerson, and Whitman, Burroughs found redemption and transcendence in Nature and the rural way of life.

WILDERSTEIN

Wilderstein, a brooding Queen
Anne-style house perched above the
Hudson River in Rhinebeck, has been
home to the Suckley family for four
generations. Miss Daisy Suckley, the last
of the Suckleys to inhabit the house,
lived there by herself until her death in
1991 at age ninety-nine. The house,
which is now a museum, went unpainted
for over seventy-five years. Miss Daisy
claimed that the last paint job in 1910
was "done with very good paint."

The sumptuous moldings of plaster and carved wood, as well as the walls covered with yellow leaded silk, are unrestored. The drawing room was lit entirely by candles, although the house had its own small hydroelectric generator installed in the 1890s.

The opulent white and gold Louis XVI drawing room is shown here in its "summer dress" of white slipcovers placed over Aubusson-style furniture. Originally a "ladies' parlor," the room has been used over the years as a billiards room and also as an office. The circular canvas painting on the ceiling, done by H. Siddons Mowbray, is of *putti* playing amidst pink clouds.

The extended family of Suckley boys would sleep in this tower room on summer nights and enjoyed photographing the picturesque river views below using some of the first Brownie cameras. The five-story tower with its curved staircase is topped with a "candle snuffer" roof and embellished with a finial crown of flames.

The Flemish Gothic-style library was one of the most used rooms in the house. Over the years, smoke from the fireplace and cigars has blackened the ceiling and walls. Miss Daisy's father read to her here in his favorite wicker chair by the fire. The stained glass windows are thought to be by LaFarge.

Family items going back over one hundred fifty years are stored throughout the house. These include Miss Daisy's personal correspondence with her cousin Franklin Delano Roosevelt, which she kept in an old suitcase under her bed. In the attic, a Dutch boy figure reposes next to skates that would have been used on the frozen Hudson River or on Wilderstein's flooded tennis courts.

The high-ceilinged butler's pantry was converted into a cheerful kitchen for Miss Daisy's use; there were no butlers at Wilderstein after the 1930s. Being very short, Miss Daisy had to use the stool to reach the sink, above which hang some of the calendar tea towels given to her each year.

The quartered, sawn oak paneling of the library was made in New York City and then brought up by river barge. A family of passionate readers, the library contains a wide range of volumes reflecting their eclectic natures and varied interests such as ice boating, bird watching, dog breeding, and the classics. Miss Daisy raised Scottie dogs and gave "Falla" to Franklin Roosevelt.

J O E
E U L A ' S
H O U S E

Black-painted columns frame the
front porch of the early 1700s stone
house in Hurley belonging to Joe Eula.
When Joe bought the house thirty years
ago he says "it looked like an old lady's
hatbox." He spent the next few years
stripping off all the extraneous embel-
lishments until he got down to the
"soul of the house." Joe is a New York
City-based artist and illustrator, renowned
for his sleek and elegant design work.

After opening up the dropped ceiling and exposing the beams, Joe bought an old chicken coop and used its wonderfully aged wood to panel the inside of the roof and to make the kitchen cabinets. He likes to do lots of simple Italian cooking here, "with vegetables and herbs as close from the garden to the plate as possible."

Daffodils that grow next to the stream running through the extensive garden have been picked and artfully arranged by Joe against the stone wall of the kitchen. The little table is a focal point of the house to which he adds a different still life composition each day, according to the season and "when and if it amuses me."

An oversized linen-covered chaise sits

next to the huge hearth Joe designed

for the kitchen. Fireplace utensils and

implements lining the walls are used for

cooking over the open fire. The land-

scape oil painting is one of a series

Joe did while "on the lam in Capri."

"Chic as hell" is the way Joe describes the Shaker prayer chair placed in his center hall. This view into the living room shows one of the mantels original to the house upon which sit pre-Columbian Mayan figurines. A wooden armchair is a piece of "street art" Joe discovered one morning on a New York City curb.

Joe situated his winter studio in this room because it gets the first morning light, which is the time of day when he does his best work. Above a drawing table is an "on loan from Joshua" black-and-white photograph of Marlene Dietrich by Milton Greene, who was Joe's partner in the 1960s. The studies of flowers on the wall are by Joe, who uses his garden and its blooms—each of which he is on speaking terms with—as a constant reference point.

Above Joe's studio worktable hang letters, notes, and mementos from his many friends, among them Andy Warhol and Diana Vreeland, as well as his sketch for a Glimmerglass Opera poster. The center hall and its stair were meticulously stripped of centuries' worth of old paint and wallpaper to show the original wood and then hand rubbed to a rich patina.

The corncrib, a potted geranium in its open window, was transformed into a summer studio for painting. In front of a spirea bush in full bloom is an old wooden column that Joe uses to train vines. He began putting in his large, beautiful garden even before he could move into his house.

CANDACE WHEELER'S PENNYROYAL COTTAGE

This summer cottage, called Pennyroyal, was built in 1883 by Candace Wheeler, the first woman in America to have her own professional design firm. Situated in the Onteora Park community above Tannersville, the shingled house, still used by her descendants, has a rustic elegance. Her plan for Onteora was to create a community of artist friends and like-minded people living in simple yet harmonious houses in an inspiring natural environment.

A comfortable, cushioned porch swing was an important part of summer living in the Catskills. Candace Wheeler created many such sitting and sleeping nooks that took full advantage of the views of the "beautiful wooded and rock-piled mountains, with the afternoon sun lying in their hollows." Living simply and much of the time out-of-doors, she drew inspiration from the native flowers and plants, using them in her textile and wallpaper designs.

The solid, plain design of the kitchen incorporates serviceability with natural grace. Simple, practical touches like the chintz curtains and the oilcloth-covered rustic table are somehow very familiar and reassuring. As Candace Wheeler said, "There is no influence so potent upon life as harmonious surroundings. . . ."

Pennyroyal's parlor looks much as it did when Candace Wheeler lived here, with its simple wicker furniture and grass cloth walls painted bright yellow. The hand-painted frieze of one of her mottoes encircles the top border of the room and begins, "Who creates a Home, creates a Potent Spirit." The painting on the door was done by daughter Dora Wheeler Keith, a successful artist and member of her mother's design collaborative which promoted decorative arts careers for women.

The very long, low dining room with its beamed ceiling and blue-painted floor was a place for friends and family to gather near the woodburning stove. The furnishings at Pennyroyal were much plainer than the designs Candace Wheeler did for commissions such as the Mark Twain house and Chester Arthur's White House. The settee in the foreground was done as part of her design for the Woman's Building at the Columbian Exposition in Chicago in 1893.

Candace Wheeler, who enjoyed living in a somewhat rustic pioneer style each summer, did not care to have indoor plumbing. This tidy bath with white beadboard walls was added after her time at Pennyroyal. The casual meeting of two sinks is indicative of a room evolving over time.

A modest yet charming bedroom with a high comfort level is an example of Candace Wheeler's belief in "tracing back sensation to its source and finding out why certain things are utterly satisfactory." Rag rugs, like this colorful one, were part of the pleasure she took in unpretentious homespun and hand-crafted items.

THE
LURE

"The Lure," an Arts & Crafts-style, brown-shingled bungalow built in 1901, is home to Tom Luciano and Dina Palin, and their son Emmet. Stone steps lead down to the Woodland Valley trout stream which, along with the nearby Beaverkill, Esopus, and Schoharie, is world-renowned for fly-fishing. The nine pure mountain streams and hidden pools of the Catskills area are a magnet for anglers and the place where American fly-fishing was born.

Tom and Dina, whose Hudson antique shop specializes in early-industrial types of lighting, have used a turn-of-the-century, "standard issue" New York City subway lamp as a fixture above their 1920s kitchen table and chairs. Dina, while researching historical colors used in bungalows, found that their kitchens usually had very bright, cheery colors, such as this lime green and tangerine combination. Cork floor tiles from Portugal were painstakingly laid down by Tom.

In the pea green dining room, French folding chairs are gathered around a Stickley oak table where "late night poker games are held." The chubby armchairs came out of a Manhattan men's club. They were re-covered in deep red velvet cut from a Brooklyn movie theater's curtain. A dentist's cabinet, which Tom embellished with some copper leafing, holds old barn lanterns.

The Douglas fir woodwork and classic Arts & Crafts ceiling beams give the living room a distinguished yet cozy, camplike feel. Above the river-stone fireplace is a series of stained glass panels "depicting important moments in pharmaceutical history which reflect early-twentieth-century near-religious belief in scientific progress." Trim red leather Deco-style banquette seats came from actress Maureen O'Sullivan's old estate in Troy.

The front porch is "a great place to sit and watch the frequent and intense thunderstorms breaking over Wittenberg Mountain." The twiggy rattan furniture from the 1930s was designed by Paul Frankl for Heywood-Wakefield. Vintage Navajo rugs from an old Adirondack lodge are casually scattered about the floor.

Throughout the house casement windows swing open to let in cooling, pine-scented breezes all summer. An American 1840s daybed and a six-sided table are elegant neighbors to the orange-painted "came-with-the-house" porch swing.

Tom and Dina wanted an extra-big kitchen sink. They found this Edwardian porcelain one with its beautifully turned legs in a shop in Hudson. An oak display stand from a nearby country general store was fashioned into a rack to hold their English platters and collection of early-nineteenth-century American glass.

BARBARA DAVIS' HOUSE

Artist and designer Barbara Davis
pioneers with her four children in a
timeworn Federal farmhouse on
twenty acres near Cherry Valley, above
the Canajoharie Creek. She chose to
move to the area because of its "funky
ambiance." The back wing, painted
blue, once housed hired hands. Shaggy
brown Norfolk and Dorset sheep are
kept as pets and for their wool.

A nineteenth-century iron urn and a bee skep sit atop a small Hepplewhite country table in the front entry hall. The table came stripped and was left that way. Barbara used a see-through Lucite shelf to hold items because it "didn't visually clutter up the space." After removing wallboard, she got down to the earlier layers of wallpaper dating from the 1820s. A Swedish side chair holds a basket filled with scarves she knitted and dyed. Neoclassical electric wall lamps were converted back to candle power.

Barbara uses the lean-to sun porch for potting plants, starting seeds, and growing lettuce all summer long. An old chair wears a striped cover she made. The black cat, whose name is Little Nora, sits on the sill above a wire plant stand.

In one corner of the kitchen, an old French wine rack is used for thermos and bottle drying. A restaurant-grade oven mitt Barbara dyed turquoise hangs from a nineteenth-century wire plate rack. The tin bread box came from an old logging camp. Walls are covered with individual panels of Hessian fabric.

In the oldest part of the house, circa 1790, Barbara uses the unheated space as a "summer sitting room" and also as a home office. She exposed the original old beams and painted them white. A Sheridan sofa is covered with an antique linen slipcover she hand dyed blue. Cushions are stuffed with straw, wool from her sheep, or a mixture of both. She customized the Ikea chandelier by adding antique crystals.

The half-moon table from New England sits beneath an old school-house chalkboard that the children use for scribbling. A jar full of rhubarb from the garden rests on a soapstone foot warmer, used here as a trivet.

In the kitchen, a post office cubbyholes cupboard holds spices and condiments above the 1940s stove that came with the house. Barbara constructed new cabinets out of old windows and used silver automobile paint on the existing metal units. The long wooden table was made by placing old floorboards on top of an old industrial worktable.

Barbara cut and stenciled her bedroom's walls with a design she saw in a Swedish museum. An embroidered antique muslin drape over the iron bedstead is an "allusion to the French Directoire period." An early-nineteenth-century "bucket bench" from New York State holds a jumble of books.

The loft bedroom, which is over the oldest part of the house, contains a French daybed for Barbara's daughter Lareina. The bed was painted white with gesso and has a yellow coverlet of nineteenth-century muslin. A drape of vintage cotton hides the closet storage space next to the little eyebrow window.

FRANK FAULKNER'S CHURCH

Built in the early 1800s, the Christ Presbyterian Church has long presided over the town of Catskill, a once-important river town on the Hudson. It is now the home of artist Frank Faulkner. The Corinthian columns were donated to the church in the 1840s by a parishioner, Charles Beach. They are believed to be identical to those that once graced Beach's legendary Catskill Mountain House Hotel.

Called the "Grand Salon," this very large room was once the manse of the adjacent Presbyterian church, and may have also served as a lyceum for educational lectures and concerts. Frank has left the space open in order to exhibit his "vast collections of curiosities." As a working artist and designer he has lived in many non-residential spaces before, including a loft in Manhattan.

The salon's alcove contains a daybed covered with a flat weave Turkish soumak rug. The portrait was done by Chester Harding, a New York society painter, around 1874. A tiny daguerreotype leans against the many layers of peeling paint and plaster, left the way Frank found it because of its patina.

Greek Revival columns such as these were constructed in a nearby Catskills workshop for many neoclassical buildings around the country, including plantation houses of the antebellum south.

Frank's Sharpei Gloria sits beneath a bust of George Washington placed atop a column. On the long library table rests an Italian gilded Empire mirror with lion's paw feet. Frank, whose tastes run from neoclassical to contemporary, says he "admires things which are classically pure, yet have a primitive elegance about them."

The space of the Grand Salon is organized around a circular Charles X French table surrounded by four chairs that were all junk shop finds. Frank, who has been "accruing this old pile of junk" for decades calls it all an example of "edited clutter." The arched alcove was used as a lecture stage when Sunday school was conducted here.

LOCUST LAWN

Locust Lawn, a Federal-period house near New Paltz, was built in 1814 for Josiah Hasbrouck. It stayed in the same family until 1958 when it was given to the Huguenot Historical Society as a public museum. Hasbrouck, while serving as a congressman in Washington under Presidents Jefferson, Madison, and Monroe, was very impressed by the new architecture he saw along the Potomac. Upon retiring to Ulster County, he decided to build this grand home in keeping with the fashionable neoclassical characteristics of the time.

In the dining room, handsome double-crossback mahogany chairs were made in a style associated with the workshop of Duncan Phyffe. The table is set with a very complete service of hand-painted porcelain. Above the mantel is a portrait of Levi Hasbrouck, who inherited the farm from his father Josiah.

An extremely rare painted floor cloth survives in the large center hall, its elegant medallion design still discernible. Esther Bevier and her sister Hylah both had their portraits painted by Ammi Phillips, the famed "Border Limner." The two women, who look so much alike, each married Hasbrouck cousins.

Family tradition states that Levi and Hylah did not send their children to the local schools; instead they were home-schooled by a tutor, apparently in this library room. Wooden shoes are a remnant of the "Colonial Revival" movement that swept the country during the nineteenth century.

The Hasbroucks had the walls of the center hall faux-marbled to look old and worn in keeping with the fashion of the time. The treatment involved rubbing lampblack and ground marble dust into wet plaster and letting it dry to a stonelike surface sheen.

The clock in one of the four upstairs bedrooms dates to about 1820. The walking sticks were used by Levi and his son while out touring the extensive farming and milling operations of Locust Lawn, considered a model and very "progressive" farm under the new Federal republic.

A Staffordshire coffee pot, Castleford cream and sugar set, and a silver spoon, all of which once belonged to the Hasbroucks, have come to rest on a window sill in the dining room. The tambour curtains frame a view of the 1738 Dutch farmhouse where the family lived before Locust Lawn was built.

SY RUTKIN'S HOUSE

Architect and owner Sy Rutkin designed this curved concrete and glass "shell house" set high on a hilltop in Roxbury. The form of the house was shaped by spraying concrete against the interior of a special airform designed to Sy's specifications. His vision was to design a house that could be built anywhere in the world for a very moderate cost.

The view of the long and open living area shows the sweeping arch of the shell's glass wall. Sy chose furniture with fluid curved lines, such as the classic butterfly chair, because "the curves echo the organic forms found in nature and have a great strength." The spiral stair leads to an upper-level studio and bedroom.

Sy uses color "like punctuation marks" to emphasize the high and wide expanse of the shell's interior. The aluminum and glass commercial-type doors are simple and efficient.

The compact galley kitchen hugs the back wall of the space and was built by local craftsmen. From the porthole windows (the kind used on ships), Sy and his wife Anne Teicher look out onto sunsets while fixing dinner. A pantry is tucked away behind the wall.

The three lower-level bedrooms have doors opening out onto the terrace; in this house "inside is outside and outside is inside," says Sy. A futon daybed and simple chair are all that is required in this guest room.

T H E
H O N E Y
F A R M

Artist Katherine Spitzhoff and web
designer Dennis Coluccio bought
this "funky old farm cottage" built in
the 1920s. It is situated on a back road
in the town of Gilboa. The former
owners, an elderly beekeeper and his
wife, sold honey, maple syrup, and
hand-made souvenirs from the
front porch. Katherine planted the
white "Disco Belle" hibiscus and
lavender in the side-yard garden.

Furnishings not found at local yard sales and auctions came up from the city tied to the roof of their vintage orange BMW. The collection includes this old cottage bench, an ancient mechanic's tool chest, and an antique hickory and willow Adirondack rocker. The wall between the old kitchen and living room was removed to open up the space.

Dennis, who enjoys scouring the countryside on weekends looking for intriguing bargains, found these five kitchen chairs for fifteen dollars at a yard sale. After re-gluing, he painted them all pistachio green. The wallpaper, with its windmill and tulip pattern, was chosen in honor of the early Dutch settlers in New York State.

Above a well-preserved gas stove, the black and yellow tile is reminiscent of a checker taxicab. Katherine and Dennis feel that "the old enameled percolators make the best coffee" and this green one is a favorite.

The upstairs bedroom has an extremely low ceiling "that takes some getting used to." The blue rose-patterned wallpaper and 1920s linoleum floor have been left intact. Kazyu, their Abyssinian show cat, naps on the tufted chenille bedspread found at a Kuntzville, Pennsylvania swap meet.

DEAN
RIDDLE'S
CABIN

Dean Riddle, a garden writer, lives year-round in a former vacation cabin built in the 1950s along Stony Clove Creek, near the town of Phoenicia. This corner of his front porch looks directly out onto the luxuriant garden he has created around the cabin. Dean found the simple wooden table in a rubbish heap, while the old green metal chair came from a salvage yard in Kingston. A McCoy vase that was his mother's contains Velvet Queen sunflowers from the garden.

The beds in the main garden are edged with cobblestones and filled with both flowers and vegetables. The hard-packed dirt paths are swept often with a broom to keep them smooth and clean. Dean found the old tire planter in the back shed and hauled it out when he first arrived. After making it the centerpiece of the garden, he planted it with Swiss chard.

The main garden next to the cabin is surrounded by a stick fence made of ash saplings that were cut by the highway department and then salvaged by Dean. He grows "Lady in Red" salvia almost every year because he loves the way the vibrant blossoms attract hummingbirds. The two stick pyramids, covered with scarlet runner beans, link overhead to form a simple arbor for the yellow Adirondack chair.

The maple bed frame was Dean's when he was a child in South Carolina. The chenille bedspread was his mother's and the heirloom patchwork quilt is one of several given to him by his Aunt Lena. A Russell Wright desk from a friend just happens to match the bed perfectly.

The living room opens onto the porch and is furnished with a comfortable '50s chair Dean found for five dollars at a yard sale. The spider-legged floor lamp belonged to a dear friend who passed away; the mirror was part of a bedroom suite his parents bought when they married in 1941.

The cabin is sided with rough-cut lumber painted barn red. Dean enjoys sitting out on the bench in the front perennial garden where he can take in the views of the mountains and the garden after a long day's work.

The deep porcelain kitchen sink was the first thing Dean noticed when he stepped into the house ten years ago and he "still loves to stand at it and wash dishes." The spice rack holds a collection of small antique pitchers. The wall lamp was found at a yard sale for one dollar.

R I V E R
V I E W
F A R M

Two artists from Manhattan spend time
fixing up this 100-year-old "ruined dairy
farm" in the country's oldest continually
farmed river valley. A freestanding
outdoor screened room is used for
bug-free dining and reading on summer
evenings. A resilient mullein plant grows
through cracks in the floor next to a
rickety collection of Adirondack chairs.
Looming over the house and river, the
huge dairy barn is now inhabited
primarily by "owls, bats, and bobcats."

In the living room are several types of "half-wrecked old rockers and chairs purchased for their fragile beauty rather than stability." Freehand Burdock, a reclusive neighbor, made the blue "what-not" shelf out of driftwood and wind-felled sycamore branches. A framed lithograph of whimsical chairs by artist friend David Chambord hangs over a red chair found in the yard after a "one-hundred-year flood."

The large round table filling the square front room is used as a desk and workbench, and for dining next to the 1920s wood cookstove. A "common brass ceiling fixture" found at a grange hall sale was sprayed flat black and hung with lead figures from old trophies. The drawing of "Frankenstein at Three Mile Island" by graffiti artist Lee Quinones is displayed in a frame made with eighty-seven spark plugs.

The library contains a bookcase made out of salvaged lumber and rusted hardware found on the banks of the Schoharie creek. An old folding wooden chair was a "gift from a squirrel-hunting buddy." The red lantern is used during the frequent power failures in the Catskills.

Morning sunlight highlights a primitive sideboard bought from auctioneer Mr. Hazlett Merry of Esperance, who insisted that they also take ten iris plants as a condition of the sale. A "cobbled-together variation of a pie safe" was constructed out of a "rusty old shot-up" Plaid Stamps sign and other materials found discarded along the side of the road. It now houses books on cookery and herbs.

Out the kitchen window is a view of the black-eyed Susan garden and the screened room. The small black raku bowl was made by "local potters up near Breakabeen." The always-changing display of bric-a-brac on the window ledge currently features a twistware vase, "stripe-y picnic" wine glasses, a tiny porcelain pixie, and a glass lantern slide photo of a waterfall.

RON SMITH'S HOUSE

Designed by its owner Ron Smith, along
with architects Deborah Weintraub and
Scott Lance, this modern residence
sits atop a mountain directly overlooking
the old resort village of Fleischmann's.
It is constructed of a one-story concrete
rectangle with a two-story mahogany
"barnlike section slicing right through it."
In the formal garden encircling the house,
Ron has planted the long arbor vitae
hedge with breaks in between the trees
in order to retain the views. He says,
"the garden is having a very geometrical
relationship with the house."

The garden shed is "just a typical Farmer Jones" prefab unit with the ceiling extended upward and to which Ron has added a wing on either side. One side contains a greenhouse; the other is a "summer room" with a porch swing. He uses the greenhouse all winter for starting seeds for his raised-bed vegetable gardens.

Ron wanted to put together a furniture collection of what he calls "the new modern classics" and to arrange each piece as one would do in an art gallery. To that end, he has kept the room very spare and used gallery lighting to accentuate every item. The '80s chaise lounge was designed by Massimo Iosa Ghini, a member of the Italian "Bolidism" movement, known for creating "furniture in motion, looking like it's ready to take off."

Ron likes to throw cocktail parties out on the patio with its magnificent view of Highmount Mountain. He designed the outdoor table for entertaining; the chairs with rubber backs and perforated metal seats are by Mario Botta. A bank built of many large, smooth river rocks edges the tranquil pond.

The bathroom has a double sink made from two cast white bronze bowls set onto a simple plywood shelf. The half-wall, tiled with Vermont quarried slate, hides a shower. Ron had a glass block wall installed so that it would seem like he was taking a shower outdoors the whole year.

The kitchen's small cooking area is set into a wall and can be neatly closed up and hidden away like a sleeper compartment on a train. The native bluestone-topped island was painted periwinkle blue and terra cotta during Ron's "postmodern period, now past." A cuckoo clock by Robert Venturi adds a Tyrolean touch.

WILDWOOD

Situated on a pine-covered hillside
overlooking Round Top Mountain, the
woodsy lodge known as "Wildwood"
has been brought back to its original
grandeur by interior designer Lynne
Stair and her husband Armin Allen.
The house is built on several levels
with many sleeping porches and a wide
wooden verandah accommodating
a large number of Adirondack chairs.
The verdant slope is terraced and
landscaped with native plants such as
echinacea, ferns, and day lilies.

The house gives one a feeling of ancient family history and contains a mix of heirloom pieces and "finds from foraging through antique shops on the weekends." Flanking the fireplace in the great room hang oval portraits of Armin's great grandparents who were from St. Paul, Minnesota. The parchment-shaded lamps came out of an old family house in Lake Geneva, Wisconsin.

A window-lined, pine-paneled passageway connects the 1895 part of the house with a great room that was added right before World War I. The kerosene lamps are lit in the evenings to cast a warm glow on the marquetry chairs from the late 1800s.

Blue and white nineteenth-century export china is displayed along a high, narrow shelf and goes well with the Chinese red-painted beadboard walls that were laid horizontally in the dining room. Hitchcock chairs sit next to a divided "Dutch" door. Over a pretty little American stenciled table hangs a Hudson River Valley landscape painting.

The smart and homelike kitchen was originally designed for servants and has been only modestly updated since. Lynne and Armin appreciate the funkiness of the 1950s metal cabinets and appliances. They've added more country touches like the vernacular signs and cheerful red-and-white gingham curtains.

The long living room retains the original log walls, with the bark still clinging to them, as well as the beamed ceiling dating from the late 1800s. The cabinet along the back wall houses some of the eighteenth-century prized porcelain in which Armin, an antiques consultant, specializes. Chinese "Dogs of Fo" from a Scottish castle decorate the stone mantle, while a stuffed owl perches on a painted wicker desk that came with the house.

SALISBURY
MANOR

Salisbury Manor, a distinctive stone house in Leeds, was built in 1730 for Abraham Salisbury. He was the grandson of Capt. Sylvester Salisbury, an officer of the British forces who took New Netherland from the Dutch in 1664. Following what they called "an arduous and lengthy search for a special home" in which to raise their triplet daughters Sydney, Samantha, and Heather, Dr. Hugh F. Butts and his wife Clementine found the stately historic house in 1980. The old stone walls outlining each side of the very long drive leading up to the house are gradually being restored.

The handsome deep-paneled cherry cabinet is one of a pair that graces the wall of the back parlor. It is believed that they were built in England for former owners Rachel and Abraham Salisbury in 1730. On an eighteenth-century English corner chair rests an ancient leather-covered pharmaceutical book providing "fascinating insights into the history of medications," says Hugh.

The eclectic grouping by the fire in the front parlor is typical of Clementine's genius for creating congenial seating arrangements for "private moments and pleasurable gatherings." The 1880s Regency game table is combined with William and Mary-style chairs and a green damask-covered Victorian barrel chair. An old African Mendi mask from Sierra Leone sits upon an Alfred Dunhill humidor.

The family's favorite room, the spacious 1760 kitchen addition, is the place where "great debates occur, parties wind up, and family problems are solved." Hardwood cut on the property is used in the early-American wood-burning stove set within the massive fireplace built in 1800. The hanging copperware collection began thirty years ago with a wedding gift and seems in keeping with the Dutch history of the area.

In the upstairs center hall, cherished photographs of family and friends go back several generations. Clementine puts a lot of thought into the arrangement of these images as a way of tracing family relationships and honoring ancestors. A montage depicts her mother, Mrs. Whitehall, who was a central figure in the lives of her offspring until her death in 1989.

JOE PESCARINO and ED MINTIENS' HOUSE

A river-stone fireplace built by an itinerant poet and stonemason is the center of this open plan house. Having been extensively remodeled over the years, it has evolved into a home for photo-stylist Joe Pescarino and writer Ed Mintiens, who moved here from Los Angeles some time ago. A comfortable old rocker brought from Cape Cod and painted "Portuguese blue" sits next to a sea captain's chest used as a table.

Nestled against a steep hillside overlooking a double waterfall near Breakabeen, this house was a sawmill in the mid-1800s. A large redwood deck below their lushly planted and terraced garden has enough privacy to allow for an outdoor shower.

The living room was painted the brightest yellow they could find at the hardware store in order to cheer things up during the long, dark Catskills winters. A green-painted schoolroom table from the 1940s is once again used for reading materials. Ceiling beams were salvaged from the original sawmill.

A primitive cupboard on the porch holds collected birds' nests and feathers found in the woods. Bundles of sage grown in the garden are used for incense. A Victorian-era bamboo easel was found at a yard sale and is now utilized as a coat rack. Wall sconces fashioned out of birch bark illuminate the porch during evening meals.

The windows of the dining area look out onto the base of the cliffside which forms a kind of natural grotto where hostas, moss, ferns, and honeysuckle proliferate. One of Joe and Ed's seasonal still lifes graces the oak table. The heirloom tomatoes came from their garden and the yellow watermelon is from a farm stand down the road.

From the screened-in porch one can hear the constant sound of the waterfalls that used to power the sawmill. The rustic picnic table is a place for summer dining, as well as a flower-arranging table. Woven rag rugs made by Joe cover the blue-painted floor.

Overleaf:
A mixture of formal and informal plantings, the hilltop garden contains both heirloom roses and native Catskills plants such as asters and goldenrod. It is bisected by twig trellises that Joe made from driftwood sticks found in the Keyserkill creek below. Water is brought up to the garden via very long hoses.

BYRDCLIFFE ARTS COLONY

Byrdcliffe Arts Colony, a utopian Arts & Crafts community, began in 1902 with the purchase of seven farms around Mt. Guardian, just outside the town of Woodstock. Its founder, wealthy Englishman Ralph Whitehead, envisioned a "brotherhood of artistic collaboration" with studios for painting, weaving, metal-working, pottery, and cabinetmaking, among other crafts. Artists, writers, and musicians who spent time here include poet Hervey White, educator John Dewey, and painter Bolton Brown, as well as Thomas Mann, Isadora Duncan, John Burroughs, Wallace Stevens, and Bob Dylan.

Eastover cottage's large open studio room has been the setting for creative expression and experimentation for almost one hundred years. A range of artists have lived and worked here, from the Trapp Family singers to The Band, painters Milton and Sally Avery, and comedian Chevy Chase.

The dark brown stained cottages were made of native hemlock in a Swiss chalet-type style, with trim painted "Byrdcliffe blue." One of thirty buildings at the colony, this cottage, called Eastover, was built in 1904 for members of the faculty of Byrdcliffe's summer art school. The Byrdcliffe Arts Colony, along with its offshoot, the Maverick Society, helped create Woodstock's mystique as a mecca for music and art.

OLANA

Olana, a fantastical Moorish-style mansion begun in 1870 near Hudson, was the home and final work of art of Frederick Edwin Church, and his wife Isabel. Church, a leading figure of the Hudson River School of painting was the great American landscape artist of the nineteenth century. He spent nearly half of his life perfecting this master-piece, whose design he based on the Arabic architecture he had seen on his travels to the Middle East.

Built around this central, cross-shaped court, Olana is filled with an exotic mélange of precious things imported from the Middle East, all skillfully chosen and harmoniously arranged. Moorish arches and doorways are profusely stenciled in Church's rich and saturated palettes. The tall perforated brass lanterns on marble-topped tables held candles or oil lamps.

The belltower of Olana, whose name means "a treasured place on high" contains a large cast iron bell, which was rung as guests came up the long, winding drive. The small balcony off Isabel Church's spacious bedroom is highly decorated with openwork Mexican tiles and multi-colored bricks laid in mosaic designs.

Church used tall, Persian-arched windows to frame to the best advantage his vistas of the Hudson River and the dim blue Catskill Mountains beyond. The oval painting was Church's first exhibited work; the one above it is a view from the site of Olana that he commissioned from painter Arthur Parton. The low, India-influenced chairs were made in the shop of Lockwood DeForest, who, along with Candace Wheeler, had been a part of Louis Tiffany's Associated Artists company.

In Isabel Church's sitting room, a daybed is placed beneath Thomas Cole's painting "The Protestant Cemetery in Rome" and some sketches done by Church. Cole, who had been Church's teacher, had his home and studio across the river in the town of Catskill. The Arabesque calligraphy surrounding the doors is decorative patterning only and contains no hidden messages.

The amber glow cast by the stenciled stair-hall window creates a dreamlike aura of another dimension and enhances the magical ambience of the Moorish style that so captivated the Churches. The stencils were cut out of black paper and then sandwiched in between two layers of glass.

In the East parlor, pierced metalwork vases and a Mexican bowl sit beneath an oil sketch Church made for his larger work entitled "After Glow." Throughout the house, artifacts from their travels are arranged like still-life paintings.

In the medieval-style dining room of Olana, the Churches assembled a gallery of copies of Old Masters paintings, which Church would sometimes retouch to suit his tastes. High vaulted ceilings and tall windows flood the gallery with light where *objets d'art* on tables and a deeply carved cassonne from Italy are displayed.

OTTO ZIEMER'S DREAM HOUSE

Just outside Woodstock is Otto
Ziemer's magic bungalow, baroquely
decorated with the flotsam and jetsam
of all manner of discarded domestic
materials. Born near Dresden, Germany
at the turn of the twentieth century,
Otto moved here in 1979 with
eighteen truckloads of salvaged
materials from his previous home in
Long Island City, which burned down.
He built the grand passageway entrance
to his home with shimmering "stained
glass" and embellished it with
thousands of "doodads," as he calls the
plastic scraps he picked up on his
bicycle excursions to the local dumps.

A "gypsy caravan" is one of the many fanciful outbuildings Otto has constructed on his property, which slopes down to meet the Sawkill Creek. A Colonial Revival apricot settee and a glass-beaded curtain come together here in an unlikely way. Otto used real wood planks from a demolished henhouse on the ceiling with faux-mahogany wood paneling on the walls.

"Americans are unable to tell their treasures from their garbage," says Otto, who recreates the splendors of Old World Europe and New York's Gilded Age with discarded elements. He is continually astonished at the things he finds thrown away, such as the ornate chandelier and French provincial telephone seen here. After acquiring hundreds of porcelain mirror backs and plastic brush handles, he put them to good use as trim for the walls. Otto fashioned the tufted leather-upholstered ceiling by hand.

In the parlor, a leather swivel-seat office chair from Manhattan sits in front of a marble fireplace mantel saved from a local ruined mansion. A rich red-velvet upholstered chair has an added fringe at the bottom and a crocheted antimacassar. The room contains photos of Old Edinburgh etched onto dinner plates.

"I only come in here once in a while, I like to keep it special," says Otto about his music room which contains dual organs and zebra skin rugs. "Each room has its own melody," he says. "My house, taken all together, makes music." His father "played music back in Germany and was a cultured man." Although Otto never learned to play music himself, he did learn three trades at his father's insistence: cabinetmaking, locksmithing, and upholstering.

Otto's afternoon visitors may be offered libations in delicate china cups at this opulent, rather psychedelic, tea bar. Crystal, mirrors, and stained glass all have a kaleidoscopic effect. As Otto says, "Beauty never ends. I am trying to make my world beautiful before I go."

MIDDLE MILL COTTAGE

In a corner of the living room at the Middle Mill Cottage, a painting from the Hudson River School hangs above a chest which hides the pewter utensils, iron pots, and old ladles used for cooking in an open fireplace. The raven was found in an antiques shop and was made in the late 1800s; after 1922 it became illegal to stuff these kinds of birds.

In a tiny library-cum-guest room, a handyman's bed, which is "smaller than it is comfortable," is tucked against one wall. Some of the beds in the house have feather ticks, and some have quilts filled with milkweed fluff. The large square-paned window overlooks the waterfalls below.

The cottage, located in a quaint, secluded village in the northern Catskills, sits above a series of waterfalls. The present owner has been in residence since 1976, after having "chased out all the raccoons and fixed the holes in the roof." He says, "many have lived here over the years, from the miller to the blacksmith and a professor who discussed Chekhov over tea. They all contributed to its aura and patina." The back porch, which overlooks the stream that powered the mill, engenders a feeling of being in a treehouse.

Wainscoting found in the oldest part of the house was replicated in the kitchen, where old floorboards were reused. The paintings are copies made by the owner of those he saw in museums but couldn't afford to buy. Table and chairs are primitive Americana.

The homeowner wanted everything in his kitchen to be "to the 1803 period of the house, yet more livable." He wanted a deep granite sink, but since "you don't find them so much anymore" he had a stonemason carve one out of a single block of granite, working it as the Shakers do. A self-described "cooking dilettante," he likes to experiment with equipment from around the world such as these Chinese woks and a Moroccan rosewater holder. The turkey wing brush, used for brushing ashes back into the fire, was made by the homeowner.

GIORDANO'S

C A B I N

The tiny cabin of Lara and Pasquale
Giordano was once a chicken coop and
then a hunter's cabin, but is now a
full-time residence for these two artists
and their daughter Anna. A seating
banquette and desk are centered on
the Forester wood-burning stove,
which provides the only heating for the
house. The fiberglass shaded desk lamp
echoes the funnel shape of one of
Lara's paintings, seen on the wall.

Pasquale searches out vintage lighting fixtures wherever he goes, sometimes finding them in highly unlikely places. He found this cool lamp right down the road at an elderly farmer's yard sale. The Arts & Crafts-style metal table has a colorful tile top. French doors were added to the cabin, creating a sense of the room expanding out onto the deck and beyond.

On the wooden deck where they grow tomatoes every summer, conch shells and potted plants are set out upon a white wire table and chairs set from the 1960s. The deck overlooks their outdoor sculpture garden at the edge of the woods in the town of Samsonville.

In the dining area of the open loftlike space, a long table and chairs by American designer Paul McCobb reflect Pasquale's interest in the mid-twentieth-century modern furniture which he collects and sells. On the walls hang works of art done by friends such as Maggi Brown and Michael Beaggy. The black-and-white floor tiles and the ceiling made of knotty pine create the look of a 1950s "rec" room.

STEPHEN SHADLEY'S HOUSE

Built as a private home in 1891, the old brick "Elizabeth House" was converted into a boarding house in the early 1900s. When interior designer Stephen Shadley first saw it, he loved the way it sat on a rise above the Catskill Creek with a view of the famous arched stone bridge in Leeds. The expansive lawn slopes down to five small tourist cabins, added in the 1930s, which nestle beneath mature maple and shag-bark hickory trees.

On the fireplace mantle in the library, a brass bookend Indian is one of a pair Stephen found and painted red. It sits in front of the mural's depiction of "Sphinx Rock," a local attraction near Haines Corners. The perforated Moroccan candlestick is one of the many "nods to Olana" seen throughout the house.

Inspired by Frederic Church's Olana and "the grandeur of the local terrain," Stephen has been painting a canvas mural on the walls of his library. The scenes of local historical tourist destinations, such as the waterfall known as Fawns Leap, were copied from early photographs of the area. Stephen says he is "on a mission to find as many pieces as possible from Greene County" for his home. He calls the rocking chair "Firehouse Empire" after finding out that it originally belonged to an old Catskills firehouse.

Stephen, who has an aversion to modern kitchens in old homes, created the look of "a Victorian kitchen as if it had been updated in the 1940s." All of the modern necessities are hidden from view. The beadboard walls, wood counter top, and glass-fronted cupboards were designed by him to go with the '40s Heywood Wakefield chairs and his collection of dark green Russell Wright "Iroquois" china.

An antique photograph on linen of a hemlock grove was placed above the mantle as a tribute to the trees that once covered the Catskill hills before the boom years of the tanning industry in the early 1800s. An English leather chair with a "real Churchill quality" and a Moroccan-style ottoman holding some vintage prints sit in front of a carved fireplace mantle that is original to the house. Neighbors visiting the house have reminisced about hearing Jimmy Durante playing the piano and singing in this room.

Stephen's own bedroom on the top floor used to be the servants' quarters and came painted this beautiful "Irish blue" color. On the bed underneath a schoolroom map of New York State are vintage fabric and Catskill "Spirit of the Pines" souvenir pillows. The patchwork quilt was made out of squares of men's suit fabric. Rustic, tree trunk bedside tables were left outside for a year to weather their finish.

In a second-floor bedroom, an Adirondack-style bed is covered with a plaid cotton Beacon blanket. Stephen says he loves the play of light thrown by a pair of tramp-art lamps, which were meticulously constructed out of hundreds of popsicle sticks. The door with the colored glass insets leads onto a small balcony overlooking the village's main street.

ACKNOWLEDGMENTS

Thanks to all the homeowners who were generous in allowing us to photograph their homes and to the following people for their help with the project:

Steve Bernstein
The Cardwells
Chef John Vargo
Douglas Curran
Michel Delsol
Judy Geib
Dr. Mabel Ginsberg
Joshua Greene
Edith, Ernie & Nick Gross
Marta Hallett
L.T.I. Photo Lab
Leslie LeFebvre
David Morton
Eric Reynal
Donna & Fima at Panorama Camera
Aldo Sampieri
Kristen Schilo
Paul Smart
Tanopah
Craig Thompson
Newell Turner
Linda & Duane Watson
Tom Wolf

HISTORIC HOUSES OPEN TO THE PUBLIC

John Burroughs Cabins (page 28)
For information on tours and nature walks at Slabsides
call: 845-384-6320
www.Johnburroughs.org

Byrdcliffe (page 160)
For information: www.woodstockguild.org

Locust Lawn (page 92)
For tour information call:
845-255-1660

Olana (page 164)
For tour information call:
518-828-0135

Wilderstein (page 36)
For tour information call:
845-876-4818

INDEX